A SIMPLE GUIDE TO
RUGBY UNION

FRANK CORR

Copyright © 2010 Frank Corr
All rights reserved.

DEDICATION

This Simple Guide is dedicated to all those who have stood
for 80 minutes or more in the cold of Winter watching
30 players engage in a form of mayhem involving an oval ball,
and wondering what on Earth is going on.

CONTENTS

Acknowledgements	Page 1
Rugby – A Simple Guide	Page 1
Little Billy Elllis	Page 2
Take the Field	Page 3
Meet the Players	Page 4
Where's the Ball ?	Page 6
Hey Ref !	Page 7
The Golden Rule	Page 8
How to Win	Page 9
Let's Play	Page 9
Tackles	Page 10
The Line Out	Page 10
The Scrum	Page 11
Kick Re-Starts	Page 13
Open Play	Page 13
Penalties and Free Kicks	Page 14
Try !	Page 15
A Sporting Life	Page 16
The Top Twenty	Page 17
The Top Tournaments	Page 18

ACKNOWLEDGMENTS

Peter Keehan came up with this idea and Tony O'Reilly suggested
how we could get it published in less than two weeks.
Conleth Adamson worked wonders with the design and
Billy Porter contributed his wisdom and
Irene her patience.

RUGBY – A SIMPLE GUIDE

Rugby Union Football - a game that millions watch but few really understand.

A game of great simplicity and stunning complexity, with a 200 page rule book which changes all the time.

If you will be watching every World Cup game, following the Six Nations, Heineken Cup or the new Robabank Super 12 - or there on the sideline yelling on a son (or daughter) playing for the school - but are not quite sure what is going on, then this is a little book for you.

Little Billy Elllis

William Webb Ellis gets the credit for creating the game of rugby, which takes its name from Rugby School where he was a student. A plaque on the wall of his school says that 'William Webb Ellis, who in fine disregard for the rules as played in his time, first took the ball in his arms and ran with it'.

That was in 1823 and the problem is that rules as such did not exist in football in England at that time. It was not until 1845 that the first rugby rules were written down by three schoolboys at the same Rugby school.

But Willie did well out of his fame. The Rugby World Cup trophy bears his name.

The game grew up in English schools and then in local clubs. The Rugby Football Union was formed in 1871 and got itself involved in a whopping row in 1895 when some clubs began to pay players. The result was a schism with the emergence of a new professional sport called Rugby League which broke away from the amateur sport. Rugby Union spread to Scotland, Wales and Ireland (where the Irish Rugby Football Union was founded in 1879) and beyond to countries like Australia, New Zealand, Japan, Italy and Georgia, all of whom played broadly similar games for many years before Rugby was codified.

The game became open to professional players in 1995.

To-day Rugby Union is played by men and women, boys and girls, in more than 100 countries across five continents.

Take the Field

Apart from the bar, the first thing you will notice on entering a rugby grounds is the playing field. This is a grass space measuring a maximum of 144 metres by 70 metres which is marked out with a white line. Two Goal Lines, 100metres apart, are marked across the space and another line, creatively called the 'Half Way Line', is marked equidistant from both Goal Lines. Two further lines are marked across the space, each 22 metres from the Goal Lines. The lines running along the side of the playing area are called 'Touch Lines, the space behind each Try Line is called the 'In Goal Area' and the back line of the playing area is called the 'Dead Ball Line'.

In addition a number of dashed lines are marked on the Ground. Two of these run across the playing area ten metres from the Half Way Line and two are marked parallel to the Touch lines at distances of 5metres and 15 metres. These lines however stop five metres from each Goal Line.

Two high Posts are erected in the centre of each Goal Line. They are placed 5.6 metres apart and are joined by a Cross Bar which is placed 3 metres from the ground.

A total of 14 flag posts, each at least 1.2m. high are placed around the perimeter of the ground including the Playing Area and In Goal Area. They mark the intersections if the various continuous lines.

RUGBY UNION PITCH PLAN

Meet the Players

Shortly before the game begins you will hear a cheer or two as the players arrive on the field. Most times there will be 22 players on each side of which 15 will start the game. These will be wearing jerseys numbered I through 15. The other seven players are substitutes and wear jerseys numbered 16 through 22. In most cases, two of these substitutes must be trained to play in the front row of the scrum. Players who start the game can be replaced by a substitute but cannot then return to the game. If they suffer an injury involving bleeding however they can be temporarily

substituted and can return when the bleeding has been stopped.
A substitute front row player can also be introduced if another front row player from that team has been sent off or to the 'sin bin' (more of this later).

Now let's look at the players who will begin the game.

They are divided into Forwards (Numbers 1 through 8) and Backs (Numbers 9 through 15). The forwards form scrums and line-outs, rucks and mauls.

Numbers 1 and 3 are probably large, burley chaps. They are called 'Prop Forwards' and they 'prop up' the Hooker (Number 2) in the front row of the scrum. One is the 'Loose Head' prop (whose head and shoulder are on the outside of the front row of the scrum) and the other is the 'Tight Head Prop' (whose head and shoulder are on the inside). The 'Hooker' is also likely to be short and squat, but there are notable exceptions like Ireland's Gerry Flannery. His job is to 'hook' the ball backwards when it is placed in the scrum and also to throw the ball into the line-out. Numbers 4 and 5 operate in the Second Row of the scrum and are called 'Locks'. They also tend to be specialist jumpers in the line-out . Numbers 6, 7 and 8 form the Back Row of the scrum, with 6 and 7 called 'flankers' and eight (with tremendous insight) called Number Eight. They tend to be powerful and fast players and get to carry the ball forward after scrums

Of course all of these forwards are also highly active in rucks, mauls and 'Open Play'. Yes - we will come to these also.

Numbers 9 and 10 are called 'Half Backs' and form a link between the forwards and the other Backs. The 'Scrum Half' (Number 9) places the ball in the scrum, collects it, if his side wins the ball and then moves the play forward. He can do this by passing to the Out Half (number 10), or another back, he can kick the ball forward or he can decide to run with it himself. Scrum halves tend to be short, snappy and elusive with high passing and kicking skills.

The Number 10 or Out Half is often regarded as the pivotal player on the team and will also very often be the principal goal kicker. He will usually be the first receiver of the ball from the scrum half following a scrum or line-out and is therefore in a position to make critical decisions. He can pass the ball on to other backs, kick it forward (sometimes into touch), chip it forward and collect the ball again or run with it himself. His strategic reading of a game can often be critical to its outcome.

Numbers 12 and 13 are called Centres . They have opportunities to carry or kick the ball forward, to pass it to other players and most significantly to tackle opponents when they have the ball. Centres are strong, fast, elusive, have advanced handling and kicking skills, are great tacklers and defenders and have the ability to capitalise on the tiniest weaknesses in the opponent's defences.

Numbers 11 and 14 are called Wingers and normally play close to the touchlines. They tend to be the fastest players on the field and to be exceptional catchers of the ball and tacklers of opponents.

Much the same can be said of Number 15 who is the Full Back. He will be called upon to catch high balls ('bombs') kicked at him by opponents, to save tries with courageous tackles and also to join in attacking moves. Full backs are also often excellent kickers.

Where's the Ball ?

The only piece of equipment needed to play Rugby Union is a rugby ball. These were originally spherical like soccer balls, but over the years were made oval for easier handling. To-day's ball is oval and has four panels. It is 280-300mm long, has end to end circumference of 740-777 mm and a width circumference of 580-620mm. It can be leather or synthetic and can be treated to make it water resistant.

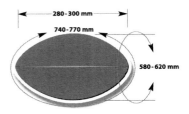

Hey Ref !

Rugby referees and officials command great respect from players and supporters, because they deserve it. They must be fully conversant with all the intricacies of the game, keep up with the play at all times and make hundreds of split-second decisions, many of which will depend on their individual interpretation of the rules.

At all rugby games the referee has two Assistants who patrol the touch lines and carry flags. They judge where the ball has left the playing area, if a penalty kick has been successful or otherwise and they can draw the attention of the referee to infringements and foul play. In many games an official Timekeeper is appointed and in televised games a Technical Match Official (TMO) is available to review the play leading to a possible try from a number of video recordings. He will answer questions put to him by the referee such as 'Is there any reason why I should not award a try ?' or 'Try - Yes or No ?'

Rugby referees communicate constantly with the players and at some games it is possible to buy little radio sets which enable spectators to hear what they are saying. They also give a range of hand signals to indicate their decisions. A raised hand for instance indicates the awarding of a penalty, a hooked hand indicates a free kick, two arms arched indicate a scrum and an extended arm indicates that a team is being given the benefit of the Advantage Rule . Most of the signals are easy to understand - so it pays to watch the referee as well as the players.

The referee has tremendous power and authority in a rugby game. He can award penalties, free kicks and scrums for foul play or infringements of the Laws and he can send players off the pitch for either a ten minute spell (to the 'Sin Bin') by showing a yellow card or for the remainder of the game by showing a Red Card.

Apart from technical breaches of the laws there are at least 40 definitions of Foul or Dangerous Play for which the referee can award a Penalty against the offending team. They include Obstruction, Intentionally or Repeatedly Offending, Time Wasting, Throwing the ball into touch, punching or striking, stamping, kicking (players - not the ball), tripping, dangerous tackling such as 'spear tackling', tackling a player who is not in possession of the ball, tackling a player whose feet are off the ground, retaliation and many others including 'dangerous play in a scrum, ruck or maul', which covers a multitude of 'sins'. Front row forwards for instance cannot 'rush' against opponents, must not intentionally (now - there's a question), lift opponents off their feet or force them upwards out of the scrum. Charging into a ruck and intentionally (again) collapsing a scrum are also 'Foul Play' offences.

The rugby referee is also the sole arbiter of the 'Advantage Law' which enables him to allow play to continue after an offence has been committed if he believes that the non-offending team can gain an advantage. If, after a period of play, he decides that no advantage has been gained, he will award the scrum, free or penalty which would have applied.

The Golden Rule

Rugby has a Golden Rule. 'Thou Shall Not Throw the Ball Forward'. Referees take a 'Zero Tolerance' approach to this rule and will penalise a player who drops the ball or who nudges it forward by a milli-zillilemetre in a maul or ruck. The rule does not apply if a kick is 'charged down'. The sanction is usually the awarding of a scrum put-in to the other side. If the knock-forward is deemed to be intentional, a penalty is awarded.

Offside is perhaps a Silver Rule. In general play, a player is 'offside' if he is in front of a team-mate who is carrying the ball, or in front of a team mate who last played the ball. Players who find themselves in an offside position can get back on-side, but they must not interfere with the play. In fact they cannot move forward or towards the ball and must get themselves at least 10 metres away from the place where the ball lands. A tall order indeed.

Offside results in the opponents getting a choice of a penalty kick or a scrum at the point where the offending team last played the ball. If this is in the 'In Goal' area the scrum will be set five metres from the Goal Line.

How to Win

Winning a rugby game is simplicity itself. All a team needs is to score more points than the opponents during the two 40 minute periods of playing time. Points can be scored by :

A Try - the Jewel in the Crown of rugby - achieved by placing the ball on the ground on the opponents goal line or in its in-goal area. This earns 5 points and the opportunity to score two further points in a Conversion. These points are scored if a player from the try-scoring team kicks the ball from the ground between the uprights and over the cross bar from a point in a direct line down the field from where the try was scored.

A Penalty Try - can be awarded by a referee if infringements by a defending side prevent a try from being scored. In this case the ball does not have to be 'grounded' and the Conversion kick is taken in front of the goal posts.

A Penalty Goal - when a team has been awarded a penalty one of its members may place the ball on the ground at the point of the infringement and try to kick it between the posts and over the cross bar. If he succeeds his team scores three points.

A Drop Goal - any player, at any point in the game, can 'drop' the ball in a straight line to the ground and kick it on the half volley. If the ball then goes between the posts and over the cross bar three points are scored.

Let's Play

A game of rugby starts with a kick-off from the centre of the half way line, with the teams previously tossing a coin to decide which has the kick, and what end of the field they will defend. Team members stay behind the kicker and charge towards their opponents once he has kicked the ball. The opposing side usually catch the ball and the game gets going. What follows is a series of players running with the ball and kicking it, tackles, line-outs, scrums, rucks, mauls, penalty kicks, free kicks, drop kicks, marked catches and hopefully some tries.

Tackles

Players rarely get to run with the ball for long before they are tackled and a whole raft of rules governs The Tackle. The laws say that rugby is to be played by players who are on their feet and therefore a player must not fall down unless of course he is tackled. A tackle occurs when the ball carrier is held by one or more opponents and both fall to the ground. It is enough however for the players to have just one knee on the ground. Once the tackle has taken place the tackler must immediately release the tackled player, get up and move away. Other players are not allowed to fall on top of them. The tackled player must try to make the ball available immediately by passing or releasing it. He cannot lie on the ball or stop opponents from gaining possession. He must also get back on his feet and move away. In the heat of battle these are difficult rules to observe and this phase result s in many penalties.

After a tackle all players playing the ball must be on their feet. They must also approach the ball from directly behind the tackle. Preventing the tackled player from passing the ball, releasing it or getting back to his feet result s in a penalty.

The Line Out

The purpose of the Line Out and the Scrum is to re-start the game in a fair manner once the ball has become unplayable. A Line Out takes place after the ball has crossed either Touch Line or is caught by a player with at least one foot in touch. Usually it is set at the point where the ball crossed the line, but there are exceptions to this rule. In open play the ball must first land within the field of play before crossing the touchline for the line-out to take place at that point. If it doesn't the line-out is set at a point parallel to where the ball was kicked. A player may however kick directly to touch from inside his own 22 metre line, but not if the ball has been passed back to him from outside that area and a Penalty can also be kicked directly into touch.

A player from the team which did not kick the ball into touch can avoid a Line Out by taking a quick throw to a team-mate provided that he is off the field of play and not nearer to the opponent's goal line than the point where the ball crossed the touch line. He must use the ball that was kicked out, throw the ball straight or towards his own goal line and for 15 metres into the field of play.

A Line Out is formed when at least two players from each team form parallel lines and stand a metre apart and between 5 and 15 metres from the touch line, facing that line. The team with the throw-in decides on the number of players it will place in the Line Out and their Opponents cannot have more than this number (they can have fewer if they wish). Players are permitted to lift team-mates who try to catch the ball or direct it back to the scrum half. The hooker throws the ball between the lines of players and the team achieving the catch or pass-back gains possession. Holding, shoving, charging, blocking and 'closing the gap' are not allowed. While the contest is supposed to be fair, the team with the throw has an advantage as it can direct the ball to specific players by calling coded signals. Players from Ireland, Wales and France like to call in their own languages.

Sometimes the hooker will throw the ball beyond the 15 metre line and if this happens his backs are allowed to run forward to contest the ball without risking off-side. The opposing backs can of course also run forward.

The Scrum

The Scrum is another means of re-starting the game, usually after a forward pass, knock on or minior rule infringement. Again it was designed to be a fair contest, but the team putting the ball into the scrum has a distinct advantage.

In what must appear to be a bizarre form of choreography, eight players from each side bind together in three rows and seek to gain advantage by pushing against each other. As we have seen, scrums are contested by forwards and each player has a specific role. When the set point of a scrum is indicated by the referee two sets of front row forwards bind together with their arms. They stand an arm's length apart and on a call from the referee they crouch, the props touch each other's outside shoulders and then withdraw their arms. A pause follows and then the referee allows them to 'engage'. This involves the loose head (left side) prop forwards getting their arm inside the right arms of their opposite numbers and grabbing their jerseys. Behind them the two Locks bind with the Props and behind them the two Flankers and our good friend the 'Number Eight' also bind. The scrum half then throws the ball into the tunnel between the two front rows and the hookers compete to 'hook' the ball backwards and out of their end of the scrum. In essence however the team with the 'put in' wins the scrum most of the time because their 'loose head' prop has a visual and ergonomic advantage.

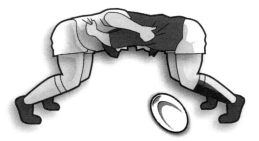

Scrummaging has well been described as the 'Black Art' of rugby and rules to prevent front rows gaining an unfair advantage have been constantly updated - only to be quickly circumvented. Penalties can be picked up for not binding correctly, obstructing the opposing scrum half, forcing a player upwards, collapsing the scrum, swinging, twisting or dipping the scrum or scrum halves straying off-side.

Kick Re-Starts

A rugby game can also be re-started with a drop kick from the centre of the half way line after the half time interval and after points have been scored. In these instances opposing players must retreat behind the 10 metre line. If a defending side grounds the ball in their in-goal area the re-start is from the 22 metre line and opposing players can take up positions up to, but not on or beyond that line. Players are also allowed to call 'Mark' if they cleanly catch a ball and are awarded a free kick under the normal rules.

Open Play

Rucks and Mauls occur during Open Play and are contests for possession of the ball. In Rucks the ball is on the ground and in Mauls it is in the hands of players.

A Ruck is formed when one or more players from each team, while on their feet, make physical contact around a ball which is on the ground. They then use their feet to try to retain or secure possession. Players joining a Ruck must bind onto a team mate or opponent using the whole arm (wrist to shoulder). Rucking players on the ground is illegal and so is falling or kneeling or intentionally collapsing the ruck. Players not involved must stay on-side (i.e behind the hindmost foot of the team-mate at the back of the ruck). If the ruck results in the ball being unplayable the referee will award a scrum to the side moving forward.

A Maul begins when a player carrying the ball is held by one or more opponents and one of his team-mates binds on the ball carrier. The minimum number of players needed to form a maul is three but in practice it is usually several more. Players joining the Maul must do so behind the foot of the hindmost team-mate. The ball-carrying team must drive forwards and stay on their feet and all players involved must be bound together. Neither side is allowed to intentionally collapse the maul. The ball can be passed back through the Maul and often ends up with the hindmost player. Those in front are not deemed to be offside provided the maul holds together as a unit. Mauls have been very difficult to defend and new rules have made defence more possible. If the ball becomes unplayable in a Maul the team moving forward is awarded a scrum. When a defender catches a high kick and is then involved in a maul and the ball becomes unplayable the defending team gets the scrum.

Penalties and Free Kicks

As we have seen, there is no shortage of opportunity to infringe the laws of rugby and therefore penalties and free kicks are a feature of every game. Penalties are awarded for serious offences (of which there are many) and they allow the non-offending team a choice of options. They can have a scrum with the put-in, they can kick to touch and also get the resultant put-in, they can tap the ball from toe to hand and run with it or they can place the ball on the ground (or on a tee) and kick for goal. If this latter kick is successful and the ball travels between the posts and over the crossbar, three points are scored.

Free kicks are awarded for lesser offences and allow the non-offending team to kick the ball from the hand or to tap it and run. Goals cannot be scored from free kicks.

Try !

This is what we come to see - the ball passed from hand to hand, a back swerving around a defender, evading a tackle and grounding the ball between the posts in the opponent's in-goal area. It does not always happen that way of course. If an attacking player is tackled just short of the line, for instance, he is allowed to use his 'momentum' to slide over the line and ground the ball, or he can stretch out his hands to ground the ball over the goal line. In either case he will have scored a try.

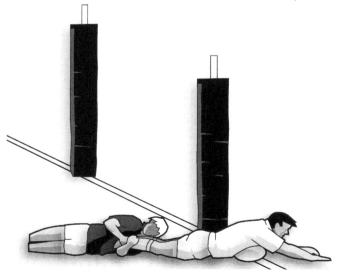

Many tries are also scored by forwards who get close to the goal line through mauls and rucks and then win a scrum. Once the ball has been placed in the scrum they can push the opposition back over the goal line and a forward can press down on the ball with his hand. Once again 'Try'. Equally forwards can force their way over the goal line with a maul or ruck and again score a touch-down Try.

The ball can be 'grounded' on or behind the Goal Line or against the goal post or its protective covering.

Tries are also often scored by Wingers. They operate very close to the touchline and often score in the corner of the in-goal area. If the player touches the corner posts (goal line or dead ball line) and is not himself in touch, a try will result.

Not all assaults on the in-goal area goal line are successful and if the attacking team infringe through a knock on or similar the defending side are awarded a scrum five metres from the goal line. This can also happen if the referee is uncertain that a try has been scored but in this case the scrum put-in is awarded to the attacking side..

A Sporting Life

Rugby has a long and proud tradition of being played in a sporting manner and this has not disappeared with the advent of professionalism. Even at the highest level players show great respect to Referees and Officials, form Guards of Honour as vanquished opponents leave the field and enjoy a level of comraderie unknown in some professional sports. This sense of Fair Play, Total Commitment, Good Fellowship and sometimes a 'healthy disregard for the rules' makes rugby what it is to-day.

Little Willie Webb Ellis would be quite proud.

The Top Twenty

The Top Twenty Rugby Nations ranked by the International Rugby Board (8th. August 2011) are:

1. New Zealand *The All Blacks*
2. Australia *The Wallabies*
3. South Africa *The Springboks*
4. England
5. France *Les Bleus*
6. Ireland
7. Wales *The Dragons*
8. Argentina *The Pumas*
9. Scotland
10. Samoa *Manu Samoa*
11. Italy *The Azzurri*
12. Japan *The Cherry Blossoms / The Brave Blossoms*
13. Tonga *Ikale Tahi*
14. Fiji *Bati*
15. Georgia *Lelos*
16. Canada *The Canucks*
17. USA *The Eagles*
18. Romania *The Oaks*
19. Russia
20. Namibia *Welwitschias*

The Top Tournaments

The top Rugby Union Tournaments are:

The Rugby World Cup - Played every four years among the top 20 national teams in the world. Some teams have to play qualifying rounds. The 2011 Rugby World Cup will be held in New Zealand in September/October.

The Six Nations Championship - This historic championship is contested annually between France, Italy, England, Ireland, Wales and Scotland. The format of the Championship involves each team playing every other team once, with home advantage alternating from one year to the next.

Two points are awarded for a win, one for a draw and none for a loss and unlike most other rugby union competitions the bonus point system is not used.

Victory in every game results in a 'Grand Slam' and back-to-back Grand Slams have been won on five occasions. England hold the record for the number of Grand Slams won with 12, followed by Wales with ten, France with nine, Scotland with three and Ireland with two.

Victory by any Home Nation (England, Ireland, Scotland, Wales) over the other three Home Nations constitutes a 'Triple Crown'.

Several individual competitions take place under the umbrella of the Six Nations tournament.

The oldest is the Calcutta Cup, which has been running since 1879 and is contested annually between England and Scotland.

The Millennium Trophy has been awarded to the winner of the game between England and Ireland with the first presented in 1988.

Since 2007, France and Italy have also contested for their own silverware - the Giuseppe Garibaldi Trophy.

The Tri Nations - The Tri Nations features Australia, New Zealand and South Africa and is regarded as the premier international competition in the Southern Hemisphere.

Beginning in 1996, as rugby became professional, it is famous for its intensity, as the All Blacks, Springboks and Wallabies have consistently been ranked as the top teams in world rugby.

The first clash between the featured nations was in 1903 on August 15, when New Zealand played Australia in Sydney winning 22-3. The trans-Tasman rivalry was made official in 1931, when Lord Bledisloe presented the Cup which bears his name for the winners of this fiercely-contested game.

In 2006 the Tri Nations marked its tenth anniversary, and was expanded to have all teams play each other three times (except in a World Cup year).

Super Rugby - It is generally regarded that South Pacific Championship was the earliest genesis for the Tri Nations. It was First contested in 1986 between Auckland, Canterbury, Wellington, Queensland, New South Wales and Fiji.

Renamed the Super Sixes a few years later, South Africa's readmission into international rugby in 1992 led an expanded Super 10 - viewed as the amateur pre-cursor to today's Super Rugby competition.

SANZAR (South Africa New Zealand Australia Rugby) administers the Super 12 and Tri Nations.

The Heineken Cup - Officially the European Championship, the Heineken Cup is played annually between 24 teams from England, Wales, Scotland, Ireland, France and Italy, who qualify through their own domestic tournaments. Four teams play each other in six pools and eight teams qualify for the knock-out stages.

The Amlin Challenge Cup - This tournament is played between 20 teams who do not qualify for the Heineken Cup but qualify through other criteria in their domestic tournaments. The five Pool winners plus three Heineken Cup Pool runners-up compete in the knock-out stages.
IRB Junior World Championship - An international championship similar to the Rugby World Cup for junior international teams.

HSBC Sevens Rugby Series - The premier international competition for Sevens Rugby.

IRB Nations Cup - A tournament for developing nations in Europe who play in seven Divisions of five to six teams on a two year cycle.

The Churchill Cup - A tournament involving international teams from England, Canada and the USA plus other nationals who participate occasionally.

The Celtic League - An international League for clubs from Ireland, Wales, Scotland and Italy.

Under 19 Rugby

Some modifications of the Laws apply when rugby is played by players under 19 years of age. Each team must have six players who can play in the front row of the scrum and a player who is substituted can replace an injured player. The scrum formation is 3-4-1 and the scrum cannot be pushed forward by more than 1.5 metres. A game consists of two periods of 35 minutes.

Sevens Rugby

This fast and spectacular variation on rugby involves just seven players on each side and a lot of running and passing of the ball. Each game lasts for two periods of 7 minutes but tournament finals can be of two period of ten minutes each. Scrums involve only three players from each side. Conversions are by drop kick rather than placed kick and after a score, the team that has scored re-starts the game with a drop kick. If a defending team touches down or makes the ball dead, their opponents get a free kick from the centre of the half way line. Two in-goal judges assist the referee

Made in the USA
Middletown, DE
26 February 2016